Presented to

My Son Patrick

On the occasion of

"Your New 1st Apartment"
With Love   From

XO _"Your Mom"_ XO

Date

April 25, 2002

Published by Barbour Publishing, Inc., P.O. Box 719, Uhrichsville, Ohio 44683
http://www.barbourbooks.com

 Member of the
Evangelical Christian
Publishers Association

Printed in China.

Favorite Holiday
TRADITIONS

Compiled by
Ellyn Sanna

BARBOUR
PUBLISHING, INC.

Christmas is coming,
The goose is getting fat,
Please put a penny in the old man's hat.
If you haven't a penny, a ha' penny will do,
If you haven't a ha' penny—God bless you!

TRADITIONAL CHILDREN'S RHYME

$\mathcal{A}$s a child, the greatest excitement of the entire year was Christmas. And it wasn't just Christmas Day itself that was so exciting. No, it was the anticipation, the happy knowledge that the culmination was drawing closer and closer as we ticked off the caroling parties, the Christmas cookies, the shopping trips, piling up tradition upon tradition, until at last that wonderful morning dawned: Christ's Birthday, a day of love and wonder and surprise.

"Christmas has become too commercialized!" we like to moan. Well, yes, it has. But just because a large part of the world is occupied with making money during the Christmas season, doesn't mean that we have to give the commercial world the power to rob us of Christmas's true meaning. We can choose to keep Christ at the center of our traditions; we can make Him welcome in our hearts, as we remember that He is truly the "reason for the season."

The Birthday of a King

Let us now go even unto Bethlehem,
and see this thing which is come to pass,
which the Lord hath made known unto us.

LUKE 2:15

Happy Birthday

What's a birthday without a birthday cake?

Every Christmas, my mother bakes a tall round cake, covered with fluffy frosting and holly decorations. In the middle of the cake she puts a single white candle. On Christmas Eve, my children gather around the table and sing "Happy Birthday" to Jesus. Their faces glow, and I know how real the Christ Child is to them at that moment. Then they eat their cake, hang their stockings by the fireplace, and go slowly up to bed, their eyes full of stars.

$\mathcal{M}$ any believe that the term Xmas is an attempt to remove Christ from Christmas. The truth, however, is that Xmas has been an abbreviation for Christmas for at least seven or eight centuries. The letter X is the same as the Greek letter Chi, the first letter in Christ. For this reason, the letter X has been a symbol for Christ for hundreds of years. Xmas was simply a shortening of the word, without the meaning having been changed at all.

A Time to Give

The gift of God is eternal life
through Jesus Christ our Lord.

ROMANS 6:23

*G*ift-giving is one of the most important of all Christmas traditions. Many times we trace this custom back to the three wise men who brought gifts to the Christ Child—but even before the Magi show up in the Christmas story, gift-giving is at the center of the narrative. Greater than any human gift is God's gift of His Son. Through Jesus, God gives us eternal life. When we have been given so much—a gift beyond human comprehension—how can we help but want to give whatever we can at the human level?

Most of all, the best gift we can give at Christmastime (and any other time) is the gift of ourselves.

The Nativity of Christ

Gift better than Himself God doth not know—
Gift better than his God no man can see;

God is my Gift, Himself He freely gave me;
God's gift am I, and none but God shall have me.

ROBERT SOUTHWELL (1561–1595)

The Wise Men

Almost no details are given in the Gospels about the wise men, although many stories and theories have grown up around them. Sometimes they are referred to as kings, sometimes as magi, but we always seem to assume that there were three of them, though the Bible doesn't actually say. The number three is taken from the number of gifts they brought.

Other stories name the wise men and locate their origins in various Eastern countries. The most popular of these stories describes them as three kings, each a different age and nationality, each bringing one of the three gifts. Their names in this version are Balthasar, Melchior, and Caspar. Whatever the truth of these details, they were important men who traveled a great distance to worship the Christ Child.

Gifts for a Newborn King

Gold is one of the most precious metals today. In the ancient world, gold was even more rare and precious than it is today. For the most part, objects of gold were owned only by royalty or nobility. And this is what the wise men brought to the Baby Jesus, probably formed into a piece of jewelry or a bowl. They brought the Christ Child one of the most valuable materials in the world at that time, wanting to give only the best to the new King of the Jews. Not only was He the King of the Jews, though; Jesus is the King of Kings and we are to give Him our best as well. Some see the wise men's gift of gold as representing money, symbolic of the fact that we, too, should support the work of Christ with our financial resources.

Frankincense, the second gift of the wise men, is a resin that comes from the frankincense tree of Arabia. It was originally considered sacred, and only the purest could approach the trees. To collect the resin, a cut is made in the trunk of the tree, and after the sap has oozed out and hardened for several months it is collected. When these lumps of resin are burned, they give off a sweet perfume. The burning of incense, frankincense in particular, has long been a part of worship. It was an ingredient in the holy anointing oil used by the Israelites in the purification of their temple and was burned as part of their grain offering. The wise men brought the Christ Child an expensive fragrance fit for the worship of God.

The last gift that the wise men presented to the Christ Child was myrrh. Like frankincense, myrrh is a resin and is obtained in the same way. Myrrh was also very expensive and used mainly by the rich. Unlike frankincense, however, the connotation is not worship but death. Myrrh was used to prepare bodies for burial. Along with other spices, it was wrapped close to the body with the burial clothes. Although we might think myrrh an unlikely gift to give a baby, the wise men were honoring the new King with another of the most precious substances of their time. And the myrrh's symbolism foretold the death of Christ for our sins.

If we, too, are wise,
we will bring the Christ Child
our hearts' greatest treasures,
laying them down at His feet
with worship and love and wonder.

A Time for Families

But as many as received him,
to them gave he power to become the sons of God,
even to them that believe on his name.

JOHN 1:12

Aside from gift-giving, simply spending time with our families is perhaps the tradition that's most central to our Christmas celebrations. We drive across the state, fly across the country, make whatever journeys we have to make to be reunited with the people who raised us, the people with whom we grew up, the people whose blood we share. And maybe even more important, it's a time when we stay away from our work lives and get a chance to simply spend time with the people we love the most, the people with whom we share a home.

It's only right that Christmas be a time for families—after all, Christ's birth is the event that broke down the walls between Jew and Gentile, between rich and poor, and between male and female. Through Christ, we are now all one family, all children of our Heavenly Father.

This Christmas, no matter what other Christmas traditions you keep, resolve to make spending time with your family the most important one. Don't get so busy that you miss this time of love and closeness. The cookies may be all made, the gifts all wrapped, the house fragrant with evergreen and spices—but what does it matter if we miss out on the gift of each other?

One family I know sets aside some time each Christmas Eve to remember those who have gone from the family. Their pictures are placed on the mantel, surrounded by evergreen, the symbol of eternal life. Family members reminisce together, sharing laughter and tears. Some people may share a letter they've written to the person now in heaven.

"I know some people think this is a morbid tradition," the mother told me. "But it isn't really. It helps us to feel that the people we miss are still a part of our family celebration. Otherwise we'd be pretending we didn't long for them to be with us, when we really do. This way our sorrow is acknowledged—and it becomes a part of our joy."

When you think about it, what better time than Christmas to affirm our belief that death is not the end? After all, the Christ Child's coming brought us eternal life.

For God so loved the world,
that he gave his only begotten Son,
that whosoever believeth in him
should not perish, but have everlasting life.

JOHN 3:16

Christmas Activities

And the Word was made flesh, and dwelt among us,
(and we beheld his glory,
the glory as of the only begotten of the Father,)
full of grace and truth.

JOHN 1:14

$\mathcal{D}$uring the centuries since Christ's birth, our world has accumulated various activities for celebrating Christmas. Some of these we still celebrate today, while others have passed into history; we hear the echoes of ancient traditions in some of our contemporary Christmas activities.

$\mathcal{H}$eap on more wood!—the wind is chill;
But let it whistle as it will,
We'll keep our Christmas merry still.

SIR WALTER SCOTT (1771–1832)

Gifts for a Newborn King

In medieval England, Christmas celebrations reached their zenith in terms of feasts and festivities. Kings and bishops attempted to best each other in the entertainments, tournaments, and banquets they held for their courts throughout the twelve days of Christmas. Each tried to be the most splendid, to put on the best feasts and merriments. One Christmas pie was nine feet in diameter, 165 pounds, and contained two bushels of flour, twenty pounds of butter, four geese, two rabbits, four wild ducks, two woodcocks, six snipes, four partridges, two neats' tongues, two curlews, six pigeons, and seven blackbirds. In the thirteenth century, Henry III butchered six hundred oxen for his Christmas feast, only a portion of the extravagant banquet he put on for his court.

By comparison, our own Christmas feasts seem quite modest. Next time someone accuses you of doing too much at Christmas, tell them about Henry III!

Still, a table laden with good food remains one of our favorite Christmas traditions. And yet, as Charles Dickens knew, the quantity of food has little to do with the quality of joy.

Wassailing

Wassailing, from an old Anglo-Saxon term meaning "be well," consisted of a house-to-house caroling party. The wassailers went around town on Christmas Eve, singing, and people invited them into their houses for something to eat and drink. The wassailers would bring holly and mistletoe to give to the people whose houses they visited, and in turn they were invited to drink from the wassail-bowl. The wassail-bowl contained a mulled punch, with spices, sugar, and apples. Today, the tradition of wassailing has carried over in the songs that mention them, as well as in traditional drinks such as eggnog and punch. Christmas caroling probably also has its roots in wassailing.

The Yule Log

The Yule log was once a popular tradition, although the custom has mostly disappeared. In medieval days, Yule logs were chosen by the family on February 2 and dried outside during the spring and summer. For those who keep the tradition in modern times, any log can be used but it is often decorated with ribbons, and sometimes with chemicals in order to produce colored flames. Originally it was lit from a piece of last year's log, although now it is simply added to a well-burning fire. The Yule log is supposed to burn to ash all the bad feelings of the previous year. (A family might want to write down on slips of paper any secret grudges each person has been holding, then throw them one by one into the Yule fire.) The Yule log has also carried over into modern days as the *bûche de Noël,* the French Christmas cake in the shape of a log.

Christmas Decorations

*Thy plants are an orchard of pomegranates,
with pleasant fruits; camphire, with spikenard,
spikenard and saffron; calamus and cinnamon,
with all trees of frankincense;
myrrh and aloes, with all the chief spices.*

SONG OF SOLOMON 4:13–14

Christmas wouldn't seem like Christmas without the decorations—the evergreen and holly, the candles and Christmas lights, the poinsettias and crèches and tinsel. These are the "clothes" Christmas traditionally wears in our world today, the scents and sights that make us think of this special time.

The decoration that has somehow found its way to the center of our traditions is the Christmas tree.

O Tannenbaum

O Christmas tree, O Christmas tree,
How lovely are your branches.
In summer sun, in winter snow,
A dress of green you always show.
O Christmas tree, O Christmas tree,
How lovely are your branches.

The Christmas Tree

One of the most common legends about the Christmas tree, also called "Christ's tree," names Martin Luther as having come up with the idea for the first decorated Christmas tree. Walking home one clear night, he looked up and saw stars shining through the branches of an evergreen tree. The picture was so beautiful to him that he brought a tree into his home and fastened candles to its branches, re-creating the scene from outside.

Throughout the centuries, many things have been used to decorate Christmas trees including apples, cakes, colored paper, tin stars, mushrooms, popcorn, and cranberries. Christmas trees did not become popular in England and America, however, until the 1840s.

In the early 1840s, Prince Albert and Queen Victoria set up a tree in Windsor Castle for the children. Prince Albert, a German, brought the custom with him from his homeland. The idea of the Christmas tree quickly became a fad in England and then developed into a tradition. In America, Christmas trees were also introduced by German immigrants. President Franklin Pierce brought the first Christmas tree into the White House in 1856, beginning a presidential tradition. Christmas trees did not become common in the average home, however, until almost the end of the nineteenth century.

Another legend concerning the origin of the Christmas tree tells of how, when Christ was born, all creation brought Him gifts. The palm tree, the olive, and the fir tree stood near the stable and discussed what they would give. The palm tree declared that he would give one of his palm leaves to fan the Christ Child in the heat of the summer. The olive stated that he would give his sweetest oil for Mary to anoint Jesus with. The fir tree had no idea what he could give and so he asked the others. Laughing, they told him he didn't have anything to give—his tears were too sticky and his needles much too scratchy. Sadly, the fir tree agreed that they were right—he had nothing that was worthy of the Christ Child.

An angel hovering close to the manger had heard their conversation, however, and was moved by the meekness of the fir tree. Night fell and as it became dark the angel asked some of the little stars to come down and to sit on the branches of the fir tree. When the Baby Jesus opened His eyes, the first thing He saw was the fir tree with the stars shining in its branches, and He smiled in delight. Later, as people began to celebrate the birth of Christ, they brought fir trees into their homes and decorated them with candles, so that they could see what the Baby Jesus had seen. And in this way the fir tree was honored for its humbleness and modesty.

The Advent Wreath

An evergreen wreath with four candles, the Advent wreath, is a tradition practiced by many Christian groups today, although it originated in the Lutheran church. These wreaths are often placed on church altars, but are sometimes set up in homes as well. On the first Sunday of Advent, four Sundays before Christmas, the first candle is lit. Another candle is lit each week, until on the Sunday before Christmas, all of the candles are finally burning. The lighting of the candles symbolizes the anticipation of the birth of Jesus, the Light of the world, born at Christmas.

Holly

Before holly became a Christmas green, it was used to decorate homes during the months of winter, bringing cheer to winter's bleakness. Later, it came to symbolize the life of Christ. The white flowers stand for His purity and lack of sin, the red berries for the blood He shed for our redemption, the prickly leaves for His crown of thorns, and the bitter bark for His suffering on the cross. These symbols make the holly a fitting decoration to be used at Christmas to remind us of the true meaning of Christmas—the Christ Who came to save us.

The Holly and the Ivy

The holly and the ivy,
When they are full well grown,
Of all the trees that are in the wood,
The holly bears the crown.

MEDIEVAL ENGLISH CAROL

The Poinsettia

A legend in Mexico explains another of our favorite Christmas decorations: the poinsettia plant. The legend tells of a small boy traveling with the wise men. He had no gift to offer the Christ Child because he was so poor, and so he prayed for a gift. Because his prayers were sincere, when he got up a brilliant scarlet plant grew at his feet. He took the flower in and presented it as a gift to the Baby Jesus.

The poinsettia was brought to the United States by Dr. Joel Roberts Poinsett, the American ambassador to Mexico during the nineteenth century. The Flower of the Holy Night has gained popularity ever since.

Mistletoe

In ancient England kisses were exchanged beneath mistletoe as the ceremonial ending of old grievances. Sprigs of mistletoe were hung over doors for the same reason, as a way of saying symbolically that the hosts wished peace to all their guests.

Somehow this custom found its way into English Christmas traditions—except that now the kisses exchanged have less to do with peacemaking and more to do with romance!

Nativity Scenes

Nativity scenes were first made popular by St. Francis of Assisi. Although they possibly existed before his time, he began the tradition of setting up large manger scenes in a community. Early in the thirteenth century, St. Francis built a full-sized nativity scene in Greccio, Italy, including live animals. His intent was to make the meaning of Christmas more real to the people. Since that time, the popularity of the nativity scene has increased throughout the centuries, especially in the more southern countries of Europe. No matter whether the manger scene is a paper cutout, a collection of intricately carved wooden figures, or a group of people and live animals, the meaning is still the same.

Why December 25th?

When the Roman emperor Constantine became a Christian in the fourth century, he is credited with establishing Christmas on December 25. In the third century, the festival of *Dies Invicti Solis* (the Day of the Invincible Sun) had been instated on this date by the emperor Aurelian. This festival was a celebration of Mithra, the Persian god of light, who was supposed to have been born out of a rock on December 25. Because Christ is symbolized by the sun ("But unto you that fear my name shall the Sun of righteousness arise with healing in his wings," Malachi 4:2), the transition of festivals was accomplished fairly easily. The worship of the Invincible Sun, Mithra, was done away with and replaced by the worship of the true Sun of Righteousness, Christ.

Boxing Day

In England and Canada and other countries associated with Britain, December 26 is a national holiday, known as Boxing Day. The name comes from the tradition of breaking open the church alms boxes on that day, in order to give the money to the poor. Another custom was to box up leftovers from the Christmas dinner to give to those who had to work on the day after Christmas, such as milkmen or bakers. Today it is simply a bank holiday and a day for the stores to hold Boxing Day sales.

The Christmas Season

The liturgical year thinks of Christmas as beginning on the first day of Advent, four Sundays before Christmas, and ending on Epiphany, January 6. Around the world, most countries begin their festivities two or three weeks before Christmas (usually on St. Nicholas' Day) and end them on Epiphany. Holland, however, starts Christmas on the last day of November, when St. Nicholas arrived by boat, and finishes on the second day of Christmas, December 26. Sweden makes the season even longer, beginning on St. Lucia's Day on December 13 and ending on January 13. Spain starts with the Feast of the Immaculate Conception (December 8) and ends on January 6. Most countries' celebrations conform to some religious custom; only the United States thinks of Christmas in terms of the number of "shopping days" between Thanksgiving and Christmas.

*N*o matter what Christmas traditions we observe, the central fact remains: Christmas is the day when we celebrate Christ's birth. The King of heaven loved us enough to be born as one of us. Reality has been changed forever, for God is no longer a far-off distant concept. Because of Jesus, He shares all the facets of our human experience. Regardless of whether we decorate our homes with evergreen and candles, tinsel and holly, each day of the year He is with us.